How to Care for Your Tropical Fish

CONTENTS

Photos by:
**Linda Lewis,
Dick Mills**

KINGDOM

©2001 by Kingdom Books PO9 5TL ENGLAND

INTRODUCTION

In this book, the sizes of the aquariums (tanks) are expressed in their capacity in litres. When tanks are sold, however, the size can be described in various different ways, such as litres or gallons; or the dimensions of the tank given in inches or centimetres. The following conversion information may be of help to you in expressing the size of your aquarium in the most convenient terms. When calculating the amount of water that your aquarium will hold, do remember that you will not be filling it completely to the top, and allow for the volume taken up by gravel, rocks and other ornaments.

- A litre is the equivalent of 1000 cubic centimetres.

- One cubic foot holds approximately 6.25 imperial gallons or 7.5 US gallons.

- 1000 cubic inches holds approximately 3.5 imperial gallons or 4.25 US gallons.

I hope you will find this book helpful in setting up your aquarium and that you will continue to enjoy being a tropical fish hobbyist for many years to come.

A shoal of Magnificent Rasboras. Like Danios, Rasboras are cyprinids.

LIVEBEARERS

Livebearers are among the most popular of the aquarium fish, particularly with beginners, because generally they are not too expensive or difficult to obtain and many of them are beautifully coloured. Livebearers are so called because they give birth to fully-formed young (fry) instead of laying eggs as do most fish.

Guppy

It is safe to say that more people have learned how to care for tropical fish by starting with the Guppy (*Poecilia reticulata*) than with any other fish. The wide tolerance and flexibility of the Guppy make it a superb fish for beginners.

Guppies have been bred in almost every conceivable colour pattern and fin shape. Unlike the wild-caught strains from South America, which are comparatively dull in colouration, commercially-bred Guppies offer an endless display of gleaming colours and long, flowing fins. It is therefore no surprise that they are just as popular with serious aquarists, as is shown by the number of international Guppy organisations.

Caring for and breeding the Guppy in the beginner's aquarium is relatively simple. Guppies thrive in a standard 50-100 litre aquarium with proper aeration and filtration. It is not at all difficult to provide suitable water requirements. Moderately hard water with a slightly alkaline pH and an aquarium heated to 24-25°C is strongly recommended.

These conditions also apply to the other livebearing species covered here.

Golden Sailfin Molly. Sailfins are not ideal community fish and prefer a warm aquarium with plenty of vegetation.

It is also very easy to prepare breeding quarters for the Guppy, as most pairs breed under normal aquarium conditions. For better results, raise the temperature of the tank a few degrees. This often speeds up the initial breeding process.

The normal gestation period of the female Guppy and the other livebearing species covered in this book is between four and six weeks. A pair of Guppies about three or four months old is usually mature enough for breeding. The number of newborn fry may range anywhere between 20 and 100. Like many fish, especially livebearers, Guppies eat their young if they find them, so the mortality rate of the young fish is high. You should supply the aquarium with fine-leaved plants to provide hiding places and shelter for the new babies. The young, active Guppies are free-swimming, with ravenous appetites. Several over-the-counter fry foods provide adequate nutrition but add some live foods, such as microworms or baby brine shrimp, to ensure proper growth and health. Adult Guppies readily accept a variety of foods, both prepared and frozen, but are especially fond of live foods.

If your main objective is to breed the fish, Guppies should be kept in tanks by themselves. Otherwise, the Guppy makes an excellent community fish when housed with small, non-aggressive tank-mates such as tetras or other livebearers.

Emperor Tetra. These small shoaling fish are a fascinating addition to the hobbyist's tank.

A male Guppy pursues the heavy female to eat the fry as they are born.

The Guppy is a superb tropical fish for beginners.

Swordtail

The Swordtail (*Xiphophorus helleri*) was given its common name because of the sword-like extension of the male's caudal fin. It originated in and around southern Mexico and is another colourful livebearer that is easy to maintain and breed. Overall, the Swordtail requires similar care to the Guppy. Nowadays there are several interesting varieties to choose from, such as the Red, Green, Black, Marigold and Tuxedo Swordtails. Other varieties of the Swordtail include the Lyretail and Hi-Fin Lyretail Sword.

The Swordtail's peaceful temperament makes it an ideal fish for beginners. Aggression is rare, although Swordtails of both sexes can be bullies. Sexing and breeding the Swordtail is relatively simple, even for the novice. The female Swordtail is capable of giving birth to as many as 150 young at one time and the fry are easy to raise and care for. Feeding the Swordtail is not difficult as it accepts all the usual aquarium foods, including flake, frozen and live foods.

A prizewinning female Swordtail. A female Swordtail can give birth to up to 150 young at one time.

Although wild specimens of the Swordtail can exceed 12cm in length, captive-bred individuals rarely reach 8cm. Their wonderful colouration more than makes up for their limited size.

Platies

The Platy (*Xiphophorus maculatus*) is usually not far behind the Swordtail in recognition and merit. This is another excellent livebearer that strongly deserves the popularity it enjoys. The Platy adds brilliant colouration to any aquarium. It is a peaceful and active fish that hardly ever shows any signs of aggression. Platies come in a wide selection of colour varieties, including reds, blues and yellows, some marked with black. The red Platy is the most commonly seen in the hobby.

Platies are reliable breeders, capable of producing broods of young at a rate of once a month. The typical Platy may produce well over 100 fry, but 60 to 80 is more common. Feed Platies the same as both the Swordtail and Guppy.

Mollies

Technically, the various species of Molly (*Poecilia*) should not be considered easy-to-maintain beginners' fish, but they remain extremely popular with new hobbyists and are covered here for that reason alone. Most livebearers prefer some salt added to their water but Mollies require a substantial salt content. A teaspoon of salt to every five litres of water is sufficient and makes keeping them much easier.

Mollies are peaceful and quite happy to live with most other aquarium occupants able to tolerate their water requirements. Hard alkaline water with a temperature between 23°C to 25°C is ideal. Provide aquarium lighting for about eight to ten hours a day and put plenty of plants in the tank. Although Mollies take most dry and frozen foods, it is essential that they have greens in their diet. Mollies require plenty of vegetation, both for food and, if a pair is bred, to protect the young fish.

The Molly is frequently bred in the home aquarium. The female's body gradually swells prior to giving birth. Given a well-planted aquarium, most Molly parents will not eat their young, which makes raising the fry easier. Different types of Mollies include the Marble, Lyretail, Balloon Body, and the popular Sailfin (*Poecilia latipinna*). The Sailfin is a very attractive species but is not an ideal community fish, preferring to be left alone in a warm aquarium with large amounts of vegetation.

Above: Liberty Molly.
Below: One-lined Pencilfish.

EGGLAYERS

There are many more egglaying than livebearing species of fish. Some lay adhesive eggs that stick to plants and some lay non-adhesive eggs that fall to the bottom of the aquarium. Egglayers are broken down into groups that correspond roughly to their taxonomic families. Many factors determine the incubation period of eggs: eggs may hatch at different rates and intervals depending on the species being bred, water temperature, lighting and general water requirements.

Tetras

Tetras (characins) are popular egglaying fish nearly always seen in the home aquarium. These pleasant, small, shoaling fish make wonderful additions to the hobbyist's tank, mainly because several species can be mixed together.

Neon Tetra

The Neon Tetra (*Paracheirodon innesi*) is a beautiful fish with an intense fluorescent blue stripe, and red and white throughout the body. Neons are very peaceful and an attractive asset to any community aquarium. Like other Tetras, their intense colouration becomes more pronounced when they are kept in a shoal of a dozen or more. The Neon accepts most flake and frozen foods and especially enjoys an occasional treat of live brine shrimp or daphnia. Do remember that these fish often become the dinner of larger species able to swallow them. Do not stock any fish that will grow large enough to pose such a threat to the Neon community.

Ternetz's Anostomus. Anastomidae, or headstanders, are shoaling fish not dissimilar to Tetras.

Neons are very difficult to spawn and beginners are not usually very successful with this; more experienced aquarists have greater success in breeding it. Neons available for purchase are imported from the Far East, where they are bred commercially.

Cardinal Tetra

The Cardinal Tetra (*Paracheirodon axelrodi*) is easily confused with the Neon Tetra. The two species are very similar, although the Cardinal has more red and blue colouration and it grows slightly larger. Like the Neon, the Cardinal will tolerate several tank companions and is an excellent community fish. An aquarium with minimal lighting and soft, slightly acidic water works best. Plant the tank with living and artificial decorative plants.

The Cardinal is not a fussy eater and accepts flake, frozen and live foods. A heated aquarium balanced between 21°C and 24°C is perfect. Cardinals are similar to the other shoaling Tetras in that a minimum of six of them should be placed together. Breeding the Cardinal is not a simple task and most attempts to breed them by the beginner are unsuccessful.

If you are searching for that extra boost in aquarium colour, both the Neon and Cardinal Tetra are wonderful choices, especially when placed in a tank furnished with dark gravel or situated in front of a black background.

Flame Tetra

The Flame Tetra (*Hyphessobrycon flammeus*) is a very beautiful and peaceful fish from Rio de Janeiro in South America. These fish are incredibly active and are not at all shy, actually preferring to be out in the open in small shoals, exhibiting themselves. The Flame Tetra likes slightly acidic water of temperature 24-25°C. A combination of flake, frozen and live foods of various types is always eagerly accepted. A balanced diet ensures maximum growth, but the Flame rarely grows over 5cm in length.

The Flame Tetra is good to start with if you are interested in breeding. It is easily accomplished and very rewarding. Spawning takes place on any fine-leaved plants in the tank, such as Myriophylum and Cabomba. Several eggs are released by the female and hatching occurs in two to three days. Once the fry begin to swim, feed finely chopped foods or infusoria.

Head-and-Tail Light Tetra

Head-and-Tail Light Tetras (*Hemigrammus ocellifer*), also known as Beacons, are widely distributed throughout the Amazon region. They are very tranquil and hardy fish, liking temperatures of 24-25°C. A neutral pH of 7.0 is adequate. Head-and-Tail Lights are easy to sex as the males have longer, more slender bodies and a streak which runs across their anal fin. They take nearly all types of flake foods but you should give them an additional feeding of frozen and live foods.

To appreciate fully why this Tetra received its common name, place a fluorescent light on top of the aquarium. This will show off the gleaming spots located above their eyes and at the base of their tails.

It is not difficult to breed the Head-and-Tail Light as long as you provide an aquarium of size 50-100 litres. Once you have selected a healthy, mature pair, you need to make very few additional preparations.

A male Swordtail. Despite the name, these fish are peaceful by nature.

Bloodfins

Bloodfins (*Aphyocharax anisitsi*) have been in the aquarium hobby for many years and are a popular addition to any tank. This is no surprise, since they make ideal community fish and require minimal tank maintenance. They are small shoaling fish that flourish in a clean, well-aerated aquarium heated to around 24°C. Bloodfins are not particularly fussy about water temperature but their brilliant red colouration shows up better in a warm, well-lit tank. Bloodfins dart swiftly around the aquarium in search for food. They are not picky eaters and accept nearly all commercially-prepared foods.

It is not too difficult to breed the Bloodfin but you have to do some preparation. Use a standard 50-litre aquarium and place some marbles on the aquarium bottom. Bloodfin eggs do not stick to plants or the aquarium glass, so fall safely into the crevices provided by the marble bedding. The adults can then be removed and the small eggs will hatch in 30 to 36 hours.

Glowlight Tetra

A popular egglayer from Guyana is the peaceful Glowlight Tetra (*Hemigrammus erythrozonus*). This is another Tetra species that cannot be fully appreciated unless it is displayed under correct aquarium lighting. A dark, decorated, well-planted aquarium will usually do the trick.

It is safe to say that the Glowlight Tetra is one of the most peaceful of all the many Tetras. Their water requirements include soft water with a slightly acidic pH, heated to 23-25°C. Like many of the Tetras, Glowlights are active shoaling fish and have been known to jump from the tank. Therefore, a covered aquarium is strongly recommended to discourage such antics.

Glowlights accept dry foods but prefer supplements, including varieties of frozen and live foods such as brine shrimp. If you want to breed, raise the aquarium water temperature to around 27°C or slightly above which should trigger spawning after 24 hours. During the spawning process semi-adhesive eggs are laid on the thick bunches of plants you have provided in the aquarium. Most fry hatch within three days and eat live foods eagerly.

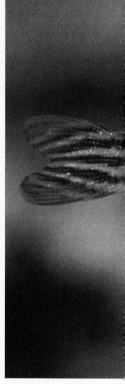

Cyprinids

Most of the cyprinids (family Cyprinidae) fall into the category of 'egg-scatterer' as far as spawning is concerned. In simple terms, these species of fish have no preference as to where their eggs are laid. Cyprinids scatter their eggs and let them lie where they fall.

Zebra Danio

Although small in number of species the genus *Brachydanio* includes two popular fish that work well in the community aquarium. The Zebra Danio (*Brachydanio rerio*) is probably the most popular egglaying fish. A community aquarium that is clean and well aerated is usually all that is needed to keep these fish successfully. This small, active shoaling fish accepts nearly all types of aquarium foods.

Breeding is also very simple and requires minimal preparation. All you need is a heated aquarium set at about 24°C. A breeding pair of Zebras will scatter non-adhesive eggs in either thick bunches of plants or over a marble bedding. The aquarium needs to contain lots of hiding places which have one purpose - to keep the parents from eating their young.

One method of sexing the Zebra Danio is by looking at the anal fin: the female has silver and blue stripes, the male gold and blue stripes.

Leopard Danio

The Leopard Danio (*Brachydanio frankei*) is another respected Brachydanio. Leopard Danios have attractive colours, are easily bred and are incredibly active in the aquarium. A standard aquarium that is aerated and filtered provides excellent living quarters for these fish. The Leopard Danio will spawn in similar fashion to the Zebra. When spawning is complete there may be as many as 1,000 eggs! Live, frozen and dried foods are willingly taken. The Leopard Danio fry are easily raised on newly-hatched live brine shrimp. Since both the Leopard Danio and Zebra Danio offer such flexibility in housing and care, they make ideal beginners' fish.

White Cloud Mountain Minnows

Among the most flexible and easy to care for of all aquarium fish are the White Cloud Mountain Minnows (*Tanichthys albonubes*). From a technical point of view they are not really tropical fish. They actually prefer a cool aquarium but are capable of living in warmer water temperatures if need be, tolerating temperatures anywhere between 18°C and 29°C. The White Cloud has a pleasant disposition and works well in most community tanks. A shoal of White Clouds can easily adapt to a small aquarium in the 30-50 litre range. They can be fed on all types of flake food, along with varieties of frozen and live foods.

The White Cloud has the reputation of being one of the easiest aquarium fish to spawn. Male and females can be kept together in a heavily-planted aquarium. They should be brought into condition on a diet of live foods and, soon afterwards, they will spawn and produce fry. White Cloud fry can be confused with the fry of Cardinals or Neons because they are very similar in colour. The fry can be fed on newly-hatched brine shrimp until they are old enough to eat other popular fish foods.

Tiger Barb

Another group of commonly-kept cyprinids comprises the fish referred to as 'Barbs'. The most desirable is the Tiger Barb (*Capoeta tetrazona*). Despite the Tiger Barbs' boisterous antics, they remain a hobby favourite, largely because of their wonderful colouration and easy breeding habits. Their only drawback is that they are inclined to nip the fins of their tank-mates, long-finned fish usually being the unfortunate victims. If you have this problem, then the best solution is to place at least a half a dozen fish to a tank. This usually results in the Tigers playfully harassing each other rather than the other fish in the tank.

Several varieties have been developed from the original standard Tiger Barb. Among these are the Albino, Blue and Moss-green. Spawning is the same for all the varieties. Equip an aquarium with plenty of vegetation, choose your pair carefully and this will usually do the trick. The Tigers prefer water that is soft and slightly acidic, with a temperature anywhere between 24°C and 29°C. For breeding purposes, an aquarium temperature in the range 28-29°C is recommended.

Young fish that are fed on infusoria and newly-hatched brine shrimp will grow rapidly if provided with adequate aquarium space. Full-grown specimens may reach over 7cm in length. You can feed adult Tiger Barbs on a variety of foods, including flake, frozen and live food. Adding more greens to the diet will enhance the adult fish's colouration and overall health. Generally speaking, Tiger Barbs may be considered good community fish as long as they are kept away from long-finned varieties such as Siamese Fighting fish or Angelfish.

This Tiger Barb is a beautiful member of the aquarium but beware: these fish sometimes like to nip the fins of their tank-mates.

White Cloud Mountain Minnow. These little shoaling fish are among the easiest to care for of all species.

Cherry Barb

The Cherry Barb (*Capoeta titteya*) is a lovely, colourful little fish that is highly popular among aquarists. This is a peaceful and undemanding fish and you will need to do little preparation to set up suitable living quarters. The Cherry's brilliant red colour intensifies during breeding and can be maintained if the fish is kept under ideal conditions. Cherry Barbs prefer a well planted tank with a slightly acidic pH of 6.6-6.8. They prefer a heated aquarium stabilised at 24-25°C. Nearly all types of aquarium foods are accepted, including flake, frozen and live foods.

A pair of Cherry Barbs need time to get used to each other but then will spawn without much difficulty. They scatter the eggs among fine-leaved plants or over the gravel bed. There may be as many as 200 young. Fry will usually hatch between 24 and 36 hours and the parents should be removed immediately since they are likely to eat their young. The Cherry Barb is a pleasant creature and a worthwhile addition to any beginner's aquarium.

Checker Barb

The Checker Barb (*Capoeta oligolepis*) is not highly coloured but has much to offer the aquarist. It is small, hardy, peaceful, easy to breed and strongly recommended for the community tank. Water composition is not critical and a slightly acid pH and temperature in the range 23-24°C is ideal. Besides taking almost all aquarium foods available, the Checker Barb will occasionally eat lettuce or spinach as a special delicacy. It has a special preference for greens in its diet and it is not unusual to see a Checker eating aquarium algae.

Distinguishing between the sexes of the Checker Barb is easy: the male is

A male Cherry Barb. These colourful little fish are popular with aquarists because they are so undemanding in their requirements.

A lively group of Checker Barbs.

darker, with a bright red-orange tinge and black markings. Both male and female have extremely large, attractive scales compared to their overall size. The Checker Barb is easy to spawn and the newborn fry are extremely small, therefore requiring very small foods.

Anabantoids

The Anabantoids are also known as labyrinth fish and are extremely popular in the hobby. They are unique in that they have a special respiratory organ that enables them to extract oxygen from the air. There are several species that make excellent community tank occupants. Many Anabantoids build bubblenests at the aquarium surface. In most cases the male Anabantoid builds the nest and single-handedly guards the young.

Siamese Fighting fish. This fish, with its long, fancy finnage, is slow swimming and should not be kept in a tank with some of the more active barbs.

Siamese Fighting Fish

One of the most widely-recognised anabantoids is the beautiful Siamese Fighting fish, also known as the Betta (*Betta splendens*). The brilliant colours and long fancy finnage of the male Siamese Fighter has made it a delight for both the beginner and the advanced hobbyist. The Siamese Fighter's ability to swim to the aquarium surface and take in air makes it possible to keep this fish in tiny tanks. Most aquarium shops do this, displaying male Siamese Fighters in small aquariums, usually of less than five-litre capacity. You should house your Siamese Fighter in a larger tank to allow more swimming space and less chance for aquarium pollutants to build up quickly.

The male Siamese Fighter is much more attractive than the female. His long, flowing fins are available in a variety of colours including blue, red, green, creamy yellow and combinations of all these colours. The females have short fins and are less colourful. Two male Siamese Fighters cannot be kept together in one aquarium, as they will fight furiously until one dies. In the community aquarium they may be placed with both livebearers and tetras. The Siamese Fighter is a slow-swimming fish and should not be placed with some of the more active Barbs.

An aquarium heated to 25-26°C is most suitable for the Siamese Fighter. It accepts various foods, including flake, frozen and live brine, shrimp, bloodworms and daphnia. Breeding the Siamese Fighter can be achieved very successfully. The male begins the spawning process by building a bubblenest at the surface of the aquarium. Once the eggs are released from the female the male takes them in his mouth and stores them in the nest. If the tank water temperature is raised by a few degrees the eggs usually hatch in two to three days. Siamese Fighter fry can be fed on infusoria, newly-hatched brine shrimp and whiteworms.

Dwarf Gourami

The Dwarf Gourami (*Colisa lalia*) is a hardy fish that adjusts extremely well to aquarium life. These fish have peaceful dispositions and rarely show any signs of aggression. The breeding habits of Dwarf Gouramis are very similar to those of the other bubblenest builders, with one exception: it builds a very deep, substantial

The Dwarf Gourami is a hardy fish with a peaceful disposition and it adjusts well to aquarium life.

Dwarf Gourami of the 'Sunset' variety.

bubblenest incorporating vegetation, twigs and other debris. In the aquarium the Dwarf Gourami flourishes in a neutral pH and should be provided with adequate amounts of natural sunlight. A water temperature range of 24-26°C is ideal for this species. Dwarfs are not fussy eaters and you can alternate live food with both frozen and dry foods.

The male Dwarf Gourami displays marvellous colour with its brilliant red irregular transverse stripes, streaked with blue. The females are more golden, with fewer stripes. As you may guess from its name, the Dwarf Gourami does not grow very big, rarely exceeding 5cm in length.

Pearl Gourami

The Pearl Gourami (*Trichogaster leeri*) is one of the most highly praised of all the Gouramis. Its magnificent colouration, combined with its undemanding aquarium needs, has made it a popular species. Water conditions are not critical. A heated aquarium around 24°C is ideal. A roomy, well-planted aquarium caters to the Pearl's somewhat shy personality. It will also like a dark gravel bed and floating plants. Pearl Gouramis have such small mouths that you should avoid feeding large pieces of food, giving only small dry and live foods.

The Pearl Gourami will spawn in the community aquarium but it is preferable to have a separate breeding tank. The size of the bubblenest and the number of eggs are both large, a thousand eggs being not uncommon. The Pearl Gourami does not indulge in the aggressive behaviour that is sometimes found in related species during spawning. Once the eggs are laid, you can remove the female, as the male tends the nest. As soon as the eggs hatch, take out the male as well. The fry should be fed on infusoria or very fine foods.

Blue Gourami

Another popular Gourami species is the Blue Gourami (*Trichogaster trichopterus*).

The Gold Gourami is a golden colour variation of the Blue, differing from the Blue in colour alone.

A large, well-heated aquarium supplied with plenty of vegetation ensures the best opportunity for a pair to spawn. A good spawning temperature is around 25°C, with a slightly acid pH. For the most part Blue Gouramis make decent community fish as long as they are not housed with fish that are too small or delicate.

Feeding the Blue Gourami is no problem. They willingly accept most foods whether dried, frozen, or live. The Blue Gourami can grow rather large in the aquarium and may well exceed 15cm in length. Therefore, as mentioned earlier, you should not put them with any small or delicate tank-mates, to prevent them from swallowing or harassing their companions.

Kissing Gourami

The Kissing Gourami (*Helostoma temmincki*) is a very difficult fish to encourage to spawn but its awkward breeding habits have not detracted from its widespread popularity in the home aquarium. Kissing Gouramis have large, protruding lips which they occasionally lock together with one another, and their common name is derived from this unique embracing action. Researchers studying these fish have

Kissing Gouramis occasionally lock their large, protruding lips with one another. Contrary to appearances, this is probably a threatening display.

come to the conclusion that this action is some type of threatening behaviour display. From a more practical point of view, the Kissing Gouramis press their lips against ornaments, plants or the glass sides of the aquarium in order to suck off the covering of slime or algae. Kissing Gouramis grow extremely large in the aquarium and therefore should be provided with spacious living quarters. For the most part they make reasonably good community fish when kept with species of their own size.

The Kissing Gourami will prosper when housed in a tank with hard water and a neutral pH. An aquarium heated to around 24°C is suitable. The Kissing Gourami is a timid fish that dislikes a brightly-lit tank, so add several floating plants to provide shade. It is a ravenous eater, requiring enormous amounts of food, usually consisting of brine shrimp, bloodworms and varieties of greens. It likes a diet rich in greens, and does well in aquariums rich in algae. If algae is unavailable, substitute lettuce or spinach. When all else fails, it hardly ever refuses basic flake food.

Cichlids

When anyone in the hobby hears the term 'cichlid', the word that immediately comes to mind is 'trouble'. Over the years, cichlids have acquired a bad reputation because they have been known to dig up the aquarium, damage plants, and fight among themselves and with other species. Contrary to popular belief, most of these problems can be solved simply by setting up suitable living quarters and learning more about the cichlids' natural habitat and general needs. Therefore, I have not summarily dismissed them as unsuitable for the first aquarium but will describe some species that are popular and often kept successfully in the hobby.

Angelfish

The Angelfish (*Pterophyllum scalare*) is recognised by every aquarist worldwide. It is probably one of the most popular egglaying cichlids ever known. Millions upon millions of tank-raised fish are sold all over the world. Several varieties of Angelfish have been produced through hybridising and fixed inbreeding. It is suitable for the community tank as long as the other inhabitants are quiet and peaceful. The Angelfish has extremely long dorsal, anal and pelvic fins that many fast-swimming, fin-nipping fish find most appetising.

A clean, heated aquarium with a temperature of around 24°C and a neutral or slightly acidic pH is most appropriate. You can feed Angelfish on most freeze-dried or live foods and they have a special liking for daphnia.

A spacious tank with ribbon-leafed plants and the right water conditions provides an ideal aquarium for spawning. Modern breeding methods include using an empty tank with no substrate, with a piece of slate or acrylic placed at an angle to provide a spawning surface for the breeding pair. In some cases, Angelfish ignore all the spawning surfaces offered and deposit eggs on filter or heater tubes. Breeding pairs can be recognised by their tendency to pair off and can later be transferred to a special tank laid out as above.

The Angelfish (*Pterophyllum scalare*). The most popular of the cichlids.

Both parents care for the eggs and the fry usually hatch after three days. The parents take great care of their young, gathering them in tight shoals at the bottom of the aquarium. Later, the fry must be fed on fine foods in the form of infusoria and newly-hatched brine shrimp.

Jack Dempsey

The Jack Dempsey (*Cichlasoma octofasciatum*) is very popular with the novice hobbyist who has a fancy for any of the larger cichlids. Its incredibly bright, light blue spots are more noticeable on the males than the females. The Jack Dempsey's tank-mates must be fish of comparable size, for it is certain to bully any smaller fish. I would not recommend the Dempsey if you are looking for a peaceful, placid fish.

The Dempseys like a large, well-decorated aquarium with plenty of rocks and driftwood as this allows for plenty of hiding places and enough area for them to establish their own territories. The water temperature should average around 24°C. The Jack Dempsey has a hearty appetite, like most of the larger cichlids. Pelleted cichlid food, beef heart, brine shrimp, and both tubifex and bloodworms are taken.

Spawning the Jack Dempsey is not difficult. The parents will thoroughly clean stones or pieces of wood before laying their eggs on them. A thousand newborn fry are not at all uncommon and they will grow very rapidly if raised on daphnia, tubifex and other finer foods.

Jack Dempsey. These fish tend to be bullies so should not be kept with smaller fish.

Oscar

The Oscar (*Astronotus ocellatus*) is one of the most popular of the larger cichlids. For some reason, aquarists often develop a special bond with this species. Oscars appear to have a more intelligent and friendly attitude towards humans than most other fish. They seem to follow their owner's every move outside the tank but probably this is due to their constant search for food rather than affection!

Albino Oscar. Oscars seem to be more conscious of human activity than most other fish.

Like the Dempsey, the Oscar must be kept with cichlids that are similar in size. Smaller, defenceless tank-mates will be harassed or, more usually, swallowed.

A spacious tank with a deep, sandy bottom decorated with rock, wood and caves will satisfy the Oscar's habitat needs. Oscars are often seen digging on the bottom of the aquarium, uprooting the plants. They are voracious fish and eat almost anything, including beef heart, dried food and any live food, such as insects.

Some of the basic types of Oscars readily available include the Red, Tiger, Black, and the newest strain, the Albino.

Blue Zebra

African cichlids are becoming more and more popular with aquarists, who consider that the intense colouration greatly resembles some of the fancy saltwater fish. The Blue Zebra (*Pseudotropheus zebra*) is certainly one of the most popular of the African cichlids. It displays magnificent colour and can be kept successfully in the home aquarium. The Blue Zebra does not grow very large but, for its size, is something of a bully. The more experienced aquarist can breed Blue Zebra more easily than the beginner.

The Blue Zebra (*Pseudotropheus zebra*) is one of the most popular of
the African cichlids.

This species is very territorial and you should give it a large, well-decorated aquarium providing adequate swimming space and plenty of room for the individual fish to establish their territories. An aquarium heated to around 26°C is ideal.

The Blue Zebra is omnivorous and requires a balanced diet of both animal and vegetable matter. They take a wide selection of aquarium foods, including bloodworms, tubifex worms, beef heart and various vegetable substances such as algae, spinach or lettuce. They also feed on basic aquarium flake foods.

The Blue zebra is a type of cichlid called a mouthbrooder. Mouthbrooders carry their eggs and young in their mouths. The newborn fry use their parents' mouths as refuges until they are capable of surviving on their own. Raise the fry on fine live foods such as baby brine shrimp.

Auratus

Another African cichlid is *Melanochromis auratus*, commonly called the Auratus. An aquarium with hard, alkaline water and a water temperature between 24°C and 27°C works best for this fish. The Auratus is a very territorial and aggressive fish and needs a large aquarium with well-secured rock structures to provide adequate retreats. The Auratus, like the Blue Zebra, is a mouthbrooder and is easily bred by the beginner.

The Auratus will accept all standard aquarium foods including frozen, freeze-dried and live food. You should also give extra feedings of vegetable matter such as algae, lettuce and spinach.

Catfish

Most beginners' tanks are incomplete without some type of Catfish. Many different families of Catfish are available for the home aquarium.

Another African cichlid is *Melanochromis auratus*, commonly called the Auratus. The Auratus is a very territorial and aggressive fish.

29

Corydoras

The most widely recognised species of Catfish belong to the genus *Corydora*. These small and peaceful Catfish are readily available and easily maintained in the home

Emerald Catfish *Brochis splendens*. A peaceful bottom dweller.

aquarium. Corys have the remarkable ability of swallowing air from the aquarium surface and absorbing its oxygen through the linings of their intestines. In the aquarium they may be resting peacefully on the gravel and suddenly, without any warning, race to the aquarium surface for a gulp of air. If you see Corys making

***Corydoras punctatus* in home aquarium.**

numerous trips to the aquarium surface, you should suspect that the water quality has begun to deteriorate.

Corys may be kept with varieties of Tetras and livebearers. A shoal of at least six Corys is best since they tend to be uneasy and shy if kept alone. A standard aquarium that is well filtered, aerated, and stocked with live plants will support most

Top: a Flagtail Porthole Catfish. Most Catfish are recognisable by their 'whiskers'.

Below: Red-tailed Catfish are often about 5cm long when they are bought but, be warned, they can grow up to 2m long!

of the Corys' needs. You must pay special attention to the type of aquarium gravel used. Sharp-edged gravel can damage the Corys' barbels. An ideal set-up is a slightly acidic pH with a heated aquarium set at 24°C. Several varieties of Corys are available and some of the more common types are the Bronze, Albino and Peppered. The Corys eagerly accept all types of flake, frozen and live foods. They also have a special liking for live bloodworms or tubifex worms.

Corys can be sexed with a great deal of accuracy as females are generally bigger and broader than the males. They have an unusual method of group spawning.

Place three males to every female in the chosen breeding tank and lower the water temperature by 2-4°C to trigger spawning. Depending on the species of Cory, eggs may be deposited on plants or flat rocks but, most often, on the sides of the tank glass. There may be as many as 700 eggs and, when hatched, the fry will accept microworms or baby brine shrimp.

Suckermouth Catfish

Suckermouth Catfish (*Hypostomus*) are often sold under the common name 'Plecostomus' or just plain 'algae eater'. Most are relatively small when sold in shops but may reach over 30cm in length when full grown. Their claim to fame is definitely not their overwhelming attractiveness but that they do an excellent job of cleaning the algae growing on aquarium glass, plants and rocks. They demand heavy

Suckermouth Catfish are very good at cleaning the tank by eating algae.

amounts of vegetable matter in their diet but they also feast on live or frozen bloodworms and tubifex worms. It should be emphasised that, without vegetable matter as the main source of their diet, the suckermouth catfish does not survive long.

Suitable water conditions include an alkaline pH (7.1-7.4) and an aquarium heated to between 24°C and 27°C. Most suckermouths are active at night, following their nocturnal instincts. Hypostomus has not been bred successfully in the home aquarium.

For the most part, small Suckermouth Catfish make perfect community fish, rarely showing signs of aggression except for an occasional dispute among themselves. On the

Live Bloodworms.

other hand, larger Suckermouth Catfish may become aggressive towards smaller tank-mates and may even be seen sucking the protective slime coating off other fish.

A Bleeding Heart Tetra, one of the many attractive varieties of these small egg-laying fish.

BIBLIOGRAPHY

MINI-ATLAS OF FRESHWATER
AQUARIUM FISHES
Dr Herbert R Axelrod and others
ISBN: 0866223851
TFH (1987)

TROPICAL FISH FOR COMMUNITY
TANKS
Waltraud Weiss
ISBN: 0866229841
TFH (1991)

TROPICAL FISH
LOOK AND LEARN
Mary E Sweeney
ISBN: 0793801702
TFH (1994)

CARE FOR YOUR TROPICAL FISH,
THE OFFICIAL RSPCA GUIDE
ISBN: 0004125487
Harper Collins (1996)

THE GUIDE TO OWNING TROPICAL
FISH
Neal Pronek
ISBN: 0793803675
TFH (1996)

HANDBOOK OF FISH DISEASES
Dieter Untergasser
ISBN: 0866227032
TFH (1998)

BUMPER GUIDE TO TROPICAL
AQUARIUM FISHES
Dick Mills
ISBN: 190238976X
Interpet (1999)